What people are saying about this book:

Read this reflection from John Stott slowly and carefully. Breathe deeply of this oxygen of faithfulness, compassion, and truth, and then live wisely and humbly in a church and world that needs such truth and grace. From the foreword by **Mark Labberton**, President of Fuller Theological Seminary, California, USA

This is magnificent: a collection of wise, biblical and thoughtful insights on a contentious topic, from a seasoned pastor and a distinguished theologian. Prescient, compassionate and true.

Andrew Wilson, Teaching Pastor at King's Church, London; and author of *Unbreakable*

John Stott remains a compelling and urgent voice in today's discussions about human sexuality, and so it is wonderful to have his work refreshed and available to the church in this format, alongside stories that underline how God's timeless word continues to bring goodness and flourishing. **Sam Allberry,** Speaker, Ravi Zacharias International Ministries; and author of *Is God Anti-Gay?*

This re-release of John Stott's work on same-sex relationships is timely, thoughtful, compassionate, and biblically compelling. He asks the right questions, and walks the reader through a theological and pastoral treatise enabling every follower of Jesus to grasp the difficulties that so many of our friends encounter.

Archbishop Foley Beach Anglican Church in North America

Truthful words continue to shi̇ ̇his issue of homosexuality are very much ̇e church tends to surrender to

Archbishop  ca

John Stott said of his book when first published: "I have sought with integrity to submit to the revelation of yesterday within the realities of today. It is not easy to combine loyalty to the past with sensitivity to the present. Yet this is our Christian calling: to live under the Word in the world". This is what we must do. I believe that the wisdom and insight the Lord gave John Stott will, through this republished work, help us to fulfil our calling in these days. I pray it will be widely read.   **Keith Sinclair,** Bishop of Birkenhead, UK

For me it has been helpful to consider the 21st century cultural scene, to revisit the key scriptural territory, and to consider how this impacts all of us in local churches, as we seek to live godly lives and proclaim the authentic Jesus to the ends of the earth.

Andy Lines, Mission Director, Crosslinks

This is a wonderful presentation of Stott's work. The contributions of personal experiences, updated information, and editor's comments underscore the real-life applicability for all Christians. It is a clear, helpful and relevant work for an important conversation.

The Rt Revd Fraser Lawton, Bishop of Athabasca, Canada

When it comes to combining truth and love without diluting either, few can match John Stott. This book carries both the theological clarity and warm, practical wisdom that Christians need to form firm convictions about the subject and to live faithfully under God's word.

Rt Revd Rennis Ponniah, Bishop of Singapore

I found these words deeply compelling when I first read them as a very young Christian, just coming to terms with my sexuality, and they remain so today. There is no better short presentation of the Bible's teaching marked, as always with John Stott's writing, by faithfulness, clarity and compassion.   **Vaughan Roberts,** President, Proclamation Trust

JOHN STOTT

SAME SEX
RELATIONSHIPS

This book is a revised and edited version of chapter 16 of *Issues Facing Christians Today* by John R.W. Stott (4th Edition) edited by Roy McCloughry and John Wyatt. Published by arrangement with The Zondervan Corporation L.L.C. a subsidiary of HarperCollins Christian Publishing, Inc.

Same-sex relationships
© John R.W. Stott/The Good Book Company 2017

This edition was revised, expanded and updated by Sean Doherty.

Published by:
The Good Book Company
Tel (US): 866 244 2165
Tel (UK): 0333 123 0880
Email (US): info@thegoodbook.com
Email (UK): info@thegoodbook.co.uk

Websites:
North America: www.thegoodbook.com
UK: www.thegoodbook.co.uk
Australia: www.thegoodbook.com.au
New Zealand: www.thegoodbook.co.nz

ISBN: 9781784982652 | Printed in the UK

Cover Design by André Parker

Contents

Foreword

by The Most Revd and Rt Hon Dr John Sentamu

ARCHBISHOP OF YORK

In the many conversations on marriage and sexuality in which, willingly or unwillingly, Anglican Christians across the world are currently engaged, it is only right that a variety of voices are heard, expressing a wide range of lived Christian experience and perspective. So I am grateful that this short chapter from Dr Stott's book *Issues Facing Christians Today*, written more than three decades ago, is being made available once again, both as a contribution to ongoing debate and as a sharing of pastoral encouragement that has been found helpful by many.

I am aware that not all will agree with his conclusions, but for me John Stott's greatest gift was his commitment to "double listening"—a practice that is an essential ingredient to proper discussion of these issues. In an interview for *Ministry Magazine* in January 1997 John Stott said:

By double listening, I mean listening, of course, to God and to the Word of God, but listening to the voices of the modern world as well. Now, I make it clear that in listening to the modern world, we are not listening with the same degree of respect as that with which we listen to the voice of God. We listen to Him in order to believe and obey what He says.

When people write to me, as they often do, complaining that, to them, it seems the church is more influenced by the moral standards of the world than by the teaching of Scripture, I have a good deal of sympathy for their unease. We cannot expect Christ and contemporary culture always to be in harmony.

However, we must not forget that we are all children of a particular time and place, and that all of us are deeply conditioned by the context of our birth and nurture. So wherever in the world we live, it is our duty as Christians, especially where there is disagreement over moral issues which affect us all, to listen with real respect to the testimonies, not only of those with whom we agree, but also of those whose experience is a challenge to us. How we read and interpret Scripture will inevitably be influenced by the experience we each bring to our reading, and we must listen both to the whole of Scripture and to Scripture as a whole.

Above all we can have confidence in the risen Christ, who promised to send the Holy Spirit to his church! To each of us God speaks, in Scripture and in life, both in compassion and with a call to holiness, and to the priorities of the kingdom. May the Holy Spirit guide us as we seek to listen to God and to the word of God, and give us grace to listen to the world also.

+Sentamu Eboracensis

Foreword

by Mark Labberton
PRESIDENT OF FULLER THEOLOGICAL SEMINARY

John Stott's writing offers disciples thoughtful oxygen for faithful Christian life. Over and over again throughout the course of his life, preaching, and writing, this was the gift that kept pouring forth from John Stott. He would be humbly grateful to hear this affirmation, but would immediately point to the source of such replenishing and renewing air in Jesus Christ, through the unique and authoritative witness of the Scriptures.

Nowhere has this air been more needed than at the many intersections of faith and culture, where sufficient oxygen can seem in low supply. The more intense, passionate and conflicted the debates over matters of life and faith, the more constricted the air supply often seems to be.

When Dr Stott first published *Issues Facing Christians Today*, this chapter on same-sex relationships was landing in a time when the public and Christian consensus about homosexual relationships was solidly and pervasively traditional. The issues were unavoidable for a person as thoughtful as John; but no one then would have imagined the sweeping shift toward a public acceptance of homosexuality that now manifests itself in both the UK and in the USA. The speed and pervasiveness of this shift throughout the world is an unprecedented social change.

In the midst of this head-spinning period, the people of God can continue to benefit greatly from what Dr Stott offers here as a biblical and theological as well as pastoral framework for same-sex issues. While denominations and congregations are currently debating, if not dividing over, these matters, this brief chapter masterfully expresses a compassionate and humane articulation of the church's historic biblical convictions.

Despite a cultural shift in attitudes toward sexuality, thoughtful Christians must continue to wrestle over such profound and intimate issues in order to allow our obedience to Christ and our faithfulness to Scripture to direct us.

Read this reflection from John Stott slowly and carefully. Breathe deeply of this oxygen of faithfulness, compassion, and truth, and then live wisely and humbly in a church and world that needs such truth and grace.

Mark Labberton

Editor's Preface

by Sean Doherty

I t's a daunting privilege for any scholar to be asked to edit an essay by so distinguished and justly admired a figure as John Stott. In my case, there was an additional reason why it felt especially so.

As a new Christian, I came to realise in my late teens that I was gay; and, not quite ready to tell anyone else yet, I wanted to know what my new-found faith said about my sexuality. Almost at random in a local Christian bookshop, I picked up a copy of *Authentic Christianity*, an anthology of Stott's writings covering a wide variety of topics.[1] I looked up homosexuality, and found an excerpt which I now know to be from the chapter on same-sex relationships in Stott's book *Issues Facing Christians Today*, which forms the basis for this book. Here is what I read:

---

1   *Authentic Christianity: From the Writings of John Stott*. Chosen and introduced by Timothy Dudley-Smith. (IVP, 1995).

We are all human beings. That is to say, there is no such phenomenon as "a homosexual". There are only people, human persons, made in the image and likeness of God, yet fallen ... However strongly we may disapprove of homosexual practices, we have no liberty to dehumanise those who engage in them.[2]

There was a further excerpt, from another publication, as follows:

Acceptance ... of a same-sex partnership rests on the assumption that sexual intercourse is "psychologically necessary" ... Christians must surely reply that it is a lie ... Authentic human fulfilment is possible without sexual experience ... Jesus himself, though unmarried, was perfect in his humanness. Same-sex friendships should of course be encouraged, which may be close, deep and affectionate. But sexual union, the "one flesh" mystery, belongs to heterosexual marriage alone.[3]

Although I still had lots of thinking and studying ahead of me, it was so helpful that the first Christian thing I ever read on the subject was clear that my identity is in Christ and not my sexuality, that my sexuality was no more fallen than anyone else's, that I am made in the image of God and that my sexuality does not undermine that, and that sex is not necessary for fulfilment.

Above all, Stott pointed me to the example of Jesus and the fact that my sexuality by no means implied that I would

---

2 *Ibid.*, p. 374.

3 *Ibid.*, pp. 374-5.

be lonely, but that I could experience deep, close and affectionate friendship—which, as I later discovered, John Stott's own personal example so visibly demonstrated. Even in these brief excerpts, there was so much that was affirming of me personally, and yet that was wonderfully Christ-centred. Even as a new Christian, I could tell they had the ring of authentic Christianity.

It was so helpful that it was in this personally affirming and Christ-centred context that I encountered not only the teaching that same-sex sexual practice is not a legitimate option for Christians, even in a loving and committed relationship, but also the rationale for such a belief: namely that sex belongs to marriage between a woman and a man as the means of joining them as "one flesh". I thank God for John Stott's warm and compassionate tone, for his conviction and clear explanation, and for the fact that *Authentic Christianity* was the book that came into my hands that day!

So, while I remain daunted, I am also thrilled that Stott's writing on same-sex unions will now enjoy a fresh lease of life—although I found it remarkably up-to-date even before editing. Reading something originally written in 1984 brings into sharp focus the fact that the arguments put forward today in favour of the church affirming same-sex relationships are not new and do not rest on fresh evidence or even fresh readings of the biblical text. It is startling to realise for just how long some of these ideas have been circulating—and indeed how roundly they were rebutted by Stott so many years ago!

Some brief comments with respect to how I went about editing the text might be in order. Indeed, why edit it at all and not simply republish it? The absolute priority was obviously to let Stott's original writing speak for itself with its characteristic vigour and warmth. I have therefore kept my interventions to a strict minimum.

However, there was a need to update Chapter 1 substantially to take account of contemporary sociological research into the incidence of homosexuality, although this does not affect the substance of what Stott says. Then, it was important to change some terminology to bring it into line with contemporary usage. I have omitted some material which was not directly relevant to Stott's argument. In one or two places I have taken the liberty of adding an update to what Stott originally wrote (and in one case registering a disagreement with his argument!), but have clearly differentiated my editorial notes from the original text.

It remains for me to thank Bishops Keith Sinclair and Timothy Dudley-Smith for their encouragement to undertake this project, Tim Thornborough of The Good Book Company for his guidance and editorial oversight, Revd Dr Chris Wright and John Stott's other literary executors for so willingly giving their approval to the project and offering some constructive suggestions, and all those who contributed their personal stories. I pray that other young gay Christians will find in this new edition that precious combination of compassion, affirmation and clarity which was of such help to me all those years ago.

1. Introduction

Few subjects have been as explosive as that of homosexuality in recent years. Rapid social change has brought about a degree of acceptance of homosexuality which is unprecedented. This has led to a change in Western perceptions of issues such as the nature of sexuality, the concept of the family, the education of our children and the nature of human rights. It is in this context that the church has to offer leadership by reflecting biblically on and responding appropriately to these questions. It does so at a time when many people see Christianity as one of the primary sources of resistance to the demand for justice and equality.

As we reflect on the message of the Bible and the demands of our culture, we need to reassert our belief in the authority of Scripture. If we waver in our belief that God has spoken to us in the Scriptures, then we are left with conjecture and opinion. Yet we also need to be sensitive to the fact that we are dealing with people's emotions, their sexual identity and their dreams of finding love and acceptance. We have a mandate to speak the truth, but we are called to speak the truth in love.

We are all human and we are all sexual. If we stereotype and stigmatise one another, then we do not treat each other with the respect that each person deserves. After all, as far as the Bible is concerned, there is no such phenomenon as "a homosexual" or "a heterosexual": there are only people made in the image of God. We all share in the glory and tragedy of being human and we share it in our sexuality as well as other areas of our lives. Whatever our ethical perspective on homosexual practice, we have no liberty to dehumanise those who engage in it. We are all frail and vulnerable and nobody has been sexually sinless apart from Jesus. Although we must not shy away from making judgments about what is right and wrong in the light of Scripture, we are not to be judgmental. We shall be judged by the standards by which we judge others. Nobody has the right to be morally superior. Besides, sexual sins are not the only sins, nor even necessarily the most sinful; pride and hypocrisy are surely worse.

In what follows, then, I want to explore what the Bible has to say about same-sex relationships from a Christian viewpoint. It may well be that some of those reading this are not Christians, but those who are will surely want to know what light Scripture can throw on this topic. Having discovered this, they will wish to seek God's grace to live in a way which is consistent with his word, obedient to his will and a witness to his world. Nevertheless, I hope that those who read this who are not Christians may hear the voice of God calling them to discover the liberty of obedience to his will in this area of their lives.

2. The Incidence of Homosexuality[4]

It is important to preface any discussion about the incidence of different forms of sexual attraction with two observations. First, it is notoriously difficult to gain accurate data in this area. Findings from population surveys are frequently flawed by biased samples or by the methodological difficulties of getting people to talk honestly about their private experiences. Methods have been refined over the years, but it is still important to reflect on any data with a degree of healthy scepticism.

Second, we need to be clear about what any one study is attempting to measure. Is it assessing feelings of attraction, actual episodes of behaviour (and if so, over what time period), or self-reported "sexual identity"? This is important because the findings of different reports vary, often markedly,

---

4 **Editor's note:** *This section has been substantially updated from Stott's original to take account of more recent studies.*

depending upon which of these indicators is being reported.

In one well-regarded US study, for example, of those women aged between 18 and 44 who defined their sexual identity as "heterosexual", 10% had had a same-sex contact; and of those who said they were "only attracted to the opposite sex" 5.5% reported having had a same-sex contact.[5]

The same study found that overall, regardless of identity label, 11.5% of all women and 5% of all men aged 25-44 had at least one same-sex sexual partner in the last year. On the other hand, a review of a range of studies carried out by the US Williams Institute found that self-reported sexual identity rates averaged only 1.8% for bisexual and 1.7% as lesbian or gay.[6]

In the UK, data from the widely cited National Surveys of Sexual Attitudes and Lifestyles (Natsal-3 for short) illustrate how reported rates have changed over time.[7] For women aged 16 to 44, the proportion who reported having had some same-sex experience rose from 4% in 1990 to 10% in 2000 and

5 A. Chandra, C. E. Copen, W. D. Mosher, "Sexual Behaviour, Sexual Attraction, and Sexual Identity in the United States: Data from the 2006-2008 National Survey of Family Growth" in "National Healthy Statistics Report" 36.3 (March 2011). Available at https://www.cdc.gov/nchs/data/nhsr/nhsr036.pdf.

6 G. J. Gates, How Many People are Lesbian, Gay, Bisexual and Transgender? Williams Institute, April 2011. Available at http://williamsinstitute.law.ucla.edu/wp-content/uploads/Gates-How-Many-People-LGBT-Apr-2011.pdf.

7 C. H. Mercer et al, "Changes in sexual attitudes and lifestyles in Britain through the life course and over time: Findings from the National Surveys of Sexual Attitudes and Lifestyles (Natsal)" in The Lancet 382 (9907), 30 November 2013: pp. 1781-94. Available at http://www.thelancet.com/pdfs/journals/lancet/PIIS0140-6736(13)62035-8.pdf.

to 16% in 2010. On the face of it this is a huge change in behaviour over just a few decades—although it could also be that women are now more ready to report what they are doing.

For self-reported sexual identity (as opposed to behaviour), the Natsal-3 data found that around 1% of women (across the whole range 16-74) and 1.5% of men said they were gay or lesbian, and a further 1.4% of women and 1% of men identified as bisexual.

These variations in rates between studies illustrate the difficulties that face researchers in finding samples of respondents who are representative of the whole population, and framing questions that that will elicit honest answers. They also illustrate the complexity of this whole question of sexual identity and orientation. Taken together with findings from longitudinal studies (which report fluidity and changeability of sexual interests in some people over time), we should be extremely cautious in reacting to simplistic assertions based upon one study.[8]

So what can we reasonably conclude?[9] In the round, the data suggest that between 2 and 4% of people (across the whole age-range) self-identify as homosexual or bisexual, but that a considerably larger proportion reports same-sex sexual experiences (with possible rates of 10-15% in women, somewhat lower for men). An even higher proportion report

---

8   For example, N. Dickson, C. Paul, P. Herbison, "Same sex attraction in a birth cohort: prevalence and persistence in early adulthood" in *Social Science and Medicine* 56.8 (2003), pp. 1607-15. This article is not available for free online, but an abstract can be found here: https://www.ncbi.nlm.nih.gov/pubmed/12639578.

9   For a comprehensive recent review by an authoritative statistician see David Spiegelhalter, *Sex by Numbers: What Statistics Can Tell Us About Sexual Behaviour.* (London: Wellcome Collection and Profile Books, 2015).

an experience of sexual attraction to people of the same sex. But we have noticed two other important points too. First, our sexual interests are much more complex and nuanced than many people today assume. The old "gay" v "straight" binary simply does not work for many people. Second, there does appear to be considerable fluidity over time for some people across the range of sexual attraction and interests, although it is also undoubtedly the case that a small proportion of the population experiences sustained and exclusive same-sex attraction from the earliest years of sexual awakening.

3. Asking the Key Question

Having laid out the context for our discussion, I am ready to ask the key question: *Are same-sex partnerships a Christian option?* I phrase my question carefully as it introduces us to three necessary distinctions.

The distinction between sins and crimes

First, at least since the Wolfenden Report of 1957 and the resultant Sexual Offences Act of 1967, we have learned to distinguish between sins and crimes. Adultery has always (according to God's law) been a sin, but in most countries it is not an offence punishable by the state. Rape, by contrast, is both a sin and a crime. The Sexual Offences Act of 1967 declared that a homosexual act performed between consenting adults over the age of twenty-one in private should no longer be a criminal offence.

However, there is a difference between decriminalising an act and legalising it. Globally, attitudes are very diverse.

Throughout Europe, following a ruling by the Court of Human Rights, laws that criminalise private consensual sex between adults are now invalid. And of course same-sex relationships have now been granted official legal recognition, first as civil partnerships (Civil Partnerships Act 2004), and in most of the UK except Northern Ireland now as marriage (Marriage [Same Sex Couples] Act 2013). Yet meanwhile, according to Australian legal scholar Professor Paula Gerber, same-sex activity is still a crime in over seventy countries around the world.[10] In many cases, it is punishable by lengthy jail sentences and other harsh treatment or even life imprisonment, and in a few cases, by execution.[11]

Sometimes this antipathy to homosexuality can threaten the very foundations of our shared humanity. At a session of the United Nations which addressed these issues, President Robert Mugabe of Zimbabwe said that lesbians and gay men are "less than human" and are, therefore, not entitled to human rights.[12] Yet human rights are those rights which are due to a human being by virtue of him or her being human and nothing else.

Editor's note: *When the Primates of the Anglican Communion agreed to discipline the Episcopal Church of the USA for its steps towards conducting same-sex marriages, they*

---

10 See the website of Professor Paula Gerber, which includes the text of the relevant law from each country: https://antigaylaws.org/all-countries-alphabetical/.

11 Ibid.

12 Cited in Brian Whitaker, "Government Disorientation", April 29, 2003, *Guardian Unlimited* https://www.theguardian.com/world/2003/apr/29/worlddispatch.gayrights [Accessed January 2017].

also "reaffirmed their rejection of criminal sanctions against same-sex attracted people." [13]

The distinction between preference and practice

Second, it is important to note from the outset that what we are concerned with here is homosexual *practice* (for which a person is responsible) and not homosexual *orientation* or preference (for which he or she is not responsible). The importance of this distinction goes beyond the attribution of responsibility to the attribution of guilt. We may not blame people for what they are, though we may for what they do. In every discussion about homosexuality we must be rigorous in differentiating between "being" and "doing"—that is, between a person's identity and activity, sexual preference and sexual practice, constitution and conduct.

Whatever our inclination, we are to bring every thought captive to Christ and recognise that sexual intercourse is a joyful celebration of the unity between one man and one woman for life. The person who cannot marry and who is living a celibate and chaste life, whatever his or her sexual orientation, is living a life which is pleasing to God.

The distinction between casual and committed

Third, we need to distinguish between casual acts and committed relationships, which (it is claimed) are just as expressive of authentic human love as is sexual intercourse in marriage between a man and a woman. No responsible homosexual person (whether Christian or not) is advocating promiscuous

---

13 http://www.primates2016.org/articles/2016/01/15/communique-primates/.

one-night stands. What some are arguing, however, such as the Lesbian and Gay Christian Movement (LGCM), is that a heterosexual marriage and a homosexual partnership are "two equally valid alternatives", being equally tender, mature and faithful.[14] The Statement of Conviction of the LGCM contains the assertion that "it is entirely compatible with the Christian faith not only to love another person of the same sex but also to express that love fully in a personal sexual relationship".[15]

The divergence between such views and the traditional teaching of the church is at the heart of a series of events which have been very painful for the Christian church. I shall mention only three. The first occurred on 28 May 2003, when Michael Ingham, Bishop of the New Westminster diocese in Canada, announced approval for six Vancouver-area parishes to bless same-sex unions. This development provoked a storm of protest within the church worldwide. The Archbishop of Canterbury, Dr Rowan Williams, said that New Westminster was "ignoring the considerable reservations of the Church" and was going "significantly further than the teaching of the Church or pastoral concern can justify". He continued, "I very much regret the inevitable tension and division that will result from this development".[16] J. I. Packer, a highly respected conservative theologian and church leader, was one of those who walked out

---

14 Malcolm Macourt (ed.), *Towards a Theology of Gay Liberation* (London: SCM Press, 1977), p. 3. The quotation comes from Mr Macourt's own introduction to the book.

15 http://www.lgcm.org.uk/about-us/what-we-believe/ [Accessed 22/2/17]

16 The full statement can be found at http://www.anglicannews.org/news/2003/05/archbishop-of-canterbury-expresses-sadness-at-new-westminster-decision.aspx.

of the synod which approved the blessing of same-sex unions. For him, it was not legitimate to allow experience to judge Scripture or to mould Scripture in order to provide a basis for the blessing of homosexual relationships.[17] Such a move deviated from biblical teaching, misled people since it did not help them to live a chaste life, and deluded people into thinking that God blesses behaviour which he condemns. He simply asked the question, "How could I do it?"

The second issue was the consecration of Rev. Canon Gene Robinson as Bishop of New Hampshire in the USA on 2 November 2003. Canon Robinson had lived in a gay relationship for fifteen years. The impact of this consecration on the global Anglican Communion was even greater than the events in New Westminster. Yet again the Archbishop of Canterbury, Rowan Williams, had to respond, and recognised in doing so that divisions were being opened up across the world as a consequence of such an event, which he called a "matter of deep regret". The consecration took place despite the fact that thirty-seven archbishops had met the previous month at Lambeth Palace and had warned of the consequences of such a move. The Archbishop's fears were confirmed when primates throughout the world expressed their disquiet and, in some cases, their sense of outrage at this development.

The third issue was the proposed appointment of Rev. Canon Dr. Jeffrey John as Bishop of Reading in the UK, which was announced on 21 May 2003 and was proposed by the Bishop of Oxford, Dr Richard Harries. Jeffrey John had been in a gay relationship for more than twenty years but said that although

---

17 J. I. Packer, "Why I Walked", *Christianity Today*, 21 January 2003.

the relationship continued, it was not now a sexual relationship; nor did he and his friend live together, because of their different ministerial responsibilities. However, he had been extremely critical of previous orthodox teaching on sexuality, especially the teaching which arose from the Lambeth Conference in 1998. Although he stated that he would abide by the teaching and discipline of the church in the area of sexuality were he to be consecrated as a bishop, many felt that there was no evidence of repentance over his previous lifestyle; nor was there sufficient confidence that he would be able to support orthodox teaching as a bishop, given his own personal views. After a meeting with Archbishop Rowan Williams, he resigned from the appointment, but was later accepted as Dean of St Albans.

These three events were extremely painful for the Church of England, and those involved, since they exposed the deep divisions which still exist on issues of human sexuality and particularly on same-sex relationships. It is important, therefore, for us as Bible-believing Christians, to examine the original text of Scripture, to see what light can be thrown on these issues.

Editor's note. *Further developments have of course followed those described above by John Stott, including the following:*
• *Consecrations of other same-sex partnered clergy as bishops.*[18]

---

18 Bishop Mary Glasspool was consecrated as suffragan bishop in the Diocese of Los Angeles in the Episcopal Church in the USA in 2010, and became a suffragan in the Diocese of New York in 2016. See http://news.bbc.co.uk/1/hi/world/americas/8684194.stm. Bishop Kevin Robertson has just been consecrated as a suffragan bishop in the Diocese of Toronto in the Anglican Church of Canada, in January 2017. See http://www.toronto.anglican.ca/2016/09/17/diocese-elects-three-new-suffragan-bishops/.

- *In 2013, the majority report of a working group on human sexuality of the House of Bishops stated that, "We do not all believe that the evidence of Scripture points to only one set of ethical conclusions [on sexuality]. In short, Christians who share an equal commitment to Scripture do not agree on the implications of Scripture for same-sex relationships".[19] It recommended that "there can be circumstances where a priest … should be free to mark the formation of a permanent same-sex relationship in a public service," although this should not use an authorised liturgy. [20]*

- *Having agreed a "provisional rite" for blessing same-sex unions in 2012, in 2015 the Episcopal Church in the USA changed its canons to remove the definition of marriage as being between a man and a woman, and authorised a marriage rite for the use of all, including same-sex couples.[21]*

- *In response, in January 2016 a meeting of Anglican primates recommended that representatives of the Episcopal Church in the USA should no longer represent the Anglican Communion "on ecumenical and interfaith bodies" and "should not be appointed or elected to an internal standing committee and … not take part in decision making on any issues pertaining to doctrine or polity." [22]*

- *In June 2016, the General Synod of the Scottish Episcopal*

---

19 *Report of the House of Bishops Working Group on Human Sexuality* (London: Church House Publishing, November 2013), para. 235, p. 70.

20 Ibid., paras. 16-17, p. 151.

21 See http://episcopaldigitalnetwork.com/ens/2015/07/01/general-convention-approves-marriage-equality/.

22 See http://www.primates2016.org/articles/2016/01/15/communique-primates/.

Church voted to initiate the process of removing from its canons the doctrinal statement that marriage is the union "of one man and one woman." [23]

- *In May 2016, Bishop Susan Goff, a suffragan bishop of the Diocese of Virginia in the Episcopal Church in the USA was appointed as "Assisting Bishop of Liverpool". This was controversial because she had voted in favour of the change to the marriage canons in America the previous year.*

- *Since the introduction of marriage for same-sex couples in the UK, a number of clergy of the Church of England have entered such marriages in contravention of the House of Bishops' Pastoral Guidance on the matter. They have been reprimanded and one in particular, Canon Jeremy Pemberton, was refused a new licence which prevented him from taking up a new post as a chaplain in the National Health Service (NHS).*

- *After Bishop Alan Wilson, the Bishop of Buckingham, had for several years been one of the few serving Church of England bishops willing to state publicly the view that the church needed to change its teaching and pastoral practice on same-sex relationships, several bishops at once contributed to the book Journeys in Grace and Truth: Revisiting Scripture and Sexuality." [24]*

The question before us, then, does not relate to homosexual practices of a casual nature, but asks whether homosexual

---

23 This represents "the first step in a process and does not represent a final decision". See http://www.scotland.anglican.org/general-synod-friday-10-june/.

24 London: ViaMedia.News and Ekklesia, 2016.

partnerships—lifelong and loving—are a Christian option. Our concern is to subject prevailing attitudes (which range from uncritical revulsion to equally uncritical endorsement) to biblical scrutiny. Has God revealed his will regarding a norm? In particular, can the Bible be shown to sanction homosexual partnerships, or at least not to condemn them? What, in fact, does the Bible condemn?

Jeanette's Story

Alice (not her real name) was everything I had ever wanted in a partner. After two previous long-term relationships and a few dalliances, I just knew that she was "it". We were destined to grow old together.

And then randomly, as a non-believer, I started reading the Bible.

When I wasn't at work, I had my head stuck in this book, and was devouring every word in front of me. During the subsequent months, although I don't recall reading any of the specific passages, I came to realise that my gay life and behaviour were simply not compatible with this holy and all-powerful God. I just knew that I couldn't become a Christian and continue with life as I knew it.

This left me in a dilemma, for I had only been attracted to my own gender since childhood. The sense of feeling different began around the age of three and only ever deepened and clarified as I entered puberty. While my friends at school started to drool over pictures of pop stars and became giddy at the sight of certain lads from the boys' school, I longed to be the recipient of their affection. I longed to love and be loved. In the 1970s, however, these were not the kind of feelings to which one could admit. I entered university at 18, finally finding other like-minded women, and soon engaged in my first physical relationship.

Over time, being gay not only felt completely natural to me, but it also became central to who I was as a person; and besides, at this particular stage in my life, I loved and was committed to Alice. The ideal scenario would be for me to become a Christian and continue actively living my life as a gay woman.

I didn't speak to anyone about my conflict, and in those days, there was precious little to read on the subject. As much as I wanted to absorb Christianity into my life, the more I read God's word, the less I was convinced that this was possible. This God, if he was who he said he was, demanded so much more than mere integration; he demanded sole rights.

And yet, I was smitten. I was being been wooed by someone who offered everything—everlasting life and love, protection and vision, peace and unfailing commitment. In return, however, this someone demanded that I lay aside all that I had ever known and commit fully to a person I hardly knew.

The angels may well have been rejoicing in heaven at the moment of my conversion, but joy was far from me. I knew that what I was doing was right, but I cried tears of sorrow knowing, at least in part, the immediate cost of taking up the cross of obedient discipleship. I walked away from Alice, the love of my life, a keenly anticipated future, and a mindset that had been fashioned over a 25-year period. My conversion to Christ happened at 2:30 am on January 23 1985.

It would be a lie to say that these past 32 years have been ones of unremitting joy. Like everyone else, my life has been a mixture of both blessings and loss. Choosing to live life in obedience to God's created order is a tough call for every believer, irrespective of orientation, attraction or marital status. But it is not an impossible call, and neither does it automatically resign a man or woman to lifelong doom and gloom. However, I haven't always found the single life to be one of endless joy and satisfaction. I have often found it to be a difficult and lonely path, especially during my 30s and early to mid-40s when my contemporaries seemed fully focused on and engaged in marriage and child-rearing. During that time, their friendships seemed forged at the school gates and via their children's friends and hobbies. It was hard not to think back to seemingly happier days (Numbers 11:5) and wonder "what if?".

But obedience to God's word truly offers a quality of life that far exceeds the cost of commitment. Denying myself the easy option of self-satisfaction has exposed the sin-infected attitudes and behaviours that are inherent in all who fall short of the glory of God (Romans 3:23), and has driven me to find solace and solution in him. This treasured relationship has opened the door to service both in my local church and all around the world.

Not long after my conversion, I read the story of the young missionary Jim Elliott, who was murdered by the indigenous Ecuadorian tribe he was trying to convert. His famous statement struck me then and has remained with me as my personal statement.

> He is no fool who gives what he cannot keep to gain that which he cannot lose.

4. Sexuality and Marriage in the Bible

The essential place to begin our investigation, it seems to me, is the institution of marriage in Genesis 2. Since many of those pressing for a more affirming attitude towards same-sex partnerships deliberately draw a parallel between them and opposite-sex marriages, it is necessary to ask whether this parallel can be justified. In his providence God has given us two distinct accounts of creation. The first (Genesis 1) is general, and affirms the equality of the sexes, since both share in the image of God and the stewardship of the earth. The second (Genesis 2) is particular, and affirms the complementarity of the sexes, which constitutes the basis for marriage being between people of the opposite sex. In this second account of creation three fundamental truths emerge.

Diverse and complementary sexes: a divine creation

First, the human need for companionship. "It is not good for the man to be alone" (Genesis 2:18). True, this assertion was later qualified when the apostle Paul (surely echoing Genesis) wrote, "It is good for a man not to have sexual relations with a woman" (1 Corinthians 7:1). That is to say, although marriage is the good institution of God, the call to singleness is also the good vocation of some. Nevertheless, as a general rule, "it is not good for the man to be alone". God has created us social beings. Since he is love, and has made us in his own likeness, he has given us a capacity to love and be loved. He intends us to live in community, not in solitude. In particular, God continued, "I will make a helper suitable for him". Moreover, this "helper" or companion, whom God pronounced "suitable for him", was also to be his sexual partner, with whom he was to become "one flesh", so that they might thereby both consummate their love and procreate their children.

Marriage between the sexes: a divine institution

Having affirmed Adam's need for a partner, the search for a suitable one began. The animals not being suitable as equal partners, a special work of divine creation took place. The sexes became differentiated. Out of the undifferentiated humanity of Adam, male and female emerged. Adam found a reflection of himself, a complement to himself, indeed a very part of himself. Having created the woman out of the man, God brought her to him. And Adam broke spontaneously into history's first love poem, saying that now at last there stood before him a creature of such beauty in herself and similarity to him that she appeared to be (as indeed she was) "made for him":

> This is now bone of my bones and flesh of my flesh; she
> shall be called "woman", for she was taken out of man.
> (Genesis 2:23)

There can be no doubting the emphasis of this story. According to Genesis 1, Eve, like Adam, was created in the image of God. But as to the manner of her creation, according to Genesis 2, she was made neither out of nothing (like the universe), nor out of "the dust of the ground" (like Adam, v 7), but out of Adam.

Fidelity within marriage: the divine intention

The third great truth of Genesis 2 concerns the resulting institution of marriage. Adam's love poem is recorded in verse 23. The "therefore" or "that is why" of verse 24 is the narrator's deduction: "That is why a man leaves his father and mother and is united to his wife, and they become one flesh".

Even the inattentive reader will be struck by the three references to "flesh": "This is ... flesh of my flesh ... they become one flesh". We may be certain that this is deliberate, not accidental. It teaches that sexual intercourse in opposite-sex marriage is more than a union; it is a kind of reunion. It is not a union of alien persons who do not belong to one another and cannot appropriately become one flesh. On the contrary, it is the union of two persons who originally were one, were then separated from each other, and now in the sexual encounter of marriage come together again.

Sexual intercourse within marriage is therefore much more than a union of bodies; it is a blending of complementary personalities through which the rich created oneness of human beings is experienced again. The complementarity of male and female sexual organs is a symbol at the physical level of a much deeper spiritual complementarity. In order to become one flesh, however, and experience this sacred mystery, certain preliminaries are necessary, which are constituent parts of marriage. "That is why" (v 24)...

- *"a man"* (*the singular indicates that marriage is an exclusive union between two individuals*)
- *"leaves his father and mother"* (*a public social occasion is in view*)
- *"and is united to his wife"* (*marriage is a loving, cleaving commitment or covenant, which is heterosexual and permanent*)
- *"and they become one flesh"* (*for marriage must be consummated in sexual intercourse, which is a sign and seal of the marriage covenant, and over which no shadow of shame or embarrassment had yet been cast*) (*v 25*).

It is of the utmost importance to note that Jesus himself later endorsed this Old Testament definition of marriage. In doing so, he both introduced it with words from Genesis 1:27 (that the Creator "made them male and female") and concluded it with his own comment ("so they are no longer two, but one flesh. Therefore what God has joined together, let no one separate", Matthew 19:6). Here, then, are three truths which Jesus affirmed:

1. sexual difference is a divine creation;
2. opposite-sex marriage is a divine institution; and
3. opposite-sex fidelity is the divine intention.

A same-sex sexual partnership is a breach of all three of these divine purposes.

The late Michael Vasey's book *Strangers and Friends* attempts to combine evangelical faith with support for same-sex partnerships.[25] In doing so he sees Genesis 2:24 as having been used to impose on Scripture the domestic ideals of the nuclear family with its "idolatry" and "self-centredness".[26] Jesus, he says, renounces marriage as part of the present world order in favour of "Christian freedom". With the family denounced as oppressive, the way is open for same-sex partnerships as another, even a better, option.

Yet he has twisted the biblical material to suit his purpose. Neither Jesus' own singleness, nor his teaching that singleness is a divine vocation for some (Matthew 19:11-12) may be taken as evidence that he opposed marriage and family, for they belong to the created order. Nor is the family envisaged in Genesis 1 and 2 as "nuclear" in a negative or selfish sense. To be sure, Jesus did inaugurate a new order, refer to his new community as his family (Mark 3:34), and warn that if an unavoidable conflict arises between our loyalty to him and our loyalty to our natural family, then our loyalty to him takes precedence (Matthew 10:37; Luke 14:26).

But Jesus and his apostles also insisted that Christians have a continuing obligation to their natural family, including reciprocal duties between parents and children, and between husbands and wives (for example, Mark 7:9-13; Ephesians 5:22 – 6:4). The new creation restores and redeems the old; it does not reject or replace it. As for idols, every good gift of God can become an idol, including marriage and family; but in themselves neither is idolatrous or enslaving. A same-sex partnership, however, is essentially incompatible with

---

25 Michael Vasey, *Strangers and Friends* (London: Hodder & Stoughton, 1995), pp. 46, 82-83.

26 Ibid., p. 116.

opposite-sex marriage as the God-ordained context for one-flesh intimacy.

Thus Scripture defines marriage as instituted by God in terms of opposite-sex monogamy. It is the union of one man with one woman, which must be publicly acknowledged (the leaving of parents), permanently sealed (the man will be "united to his wife") and physically consummated ("one flesh"). And Scripture endorses no other kind of marriage or sexual intercourse, for God provided no alternative.

Christians should not therefore single out same-sex sexual intercourse for special condemnation. The fact is that every kind of sexual relationship and activity which deviates from God's revealed intention is *ipso facto* displeasing to him and under his judgment. This includes polygamy and polyandry (which infringe the "one man, one woman" principle), cohabitation and clandestine unions (since these have involved no decisive public leaving of parents), casual encounters and temporary liaisons, adultery and many divorces (which conflict with "cleaving" and with Jesus' prohibition, "Let no one separate"), and same-sex partnerships (which violate the statement that "a man" shall be joined to "his wife").

In sum, the only one-flesh experience which God intends and Scripture affirms is the sexual union of a man with his wife, whom he recognises as "flesh of his flesh". As Rowan Williams, the previous Archbishop of Canterbury, said in his presidential address at the 13th meeting of the Anglican Consultative Council on 20 June 2005,

> Where there is a strong scriptural presumption against
> change, a long consensus of teaching in Christian history,
> and a widespread ecumenical agreement, it may well be

thought that change would need an exceptionally strong critical mass to justify it.[27]

---

27 http://rowanwilliams.archbishopofcanterbury.org/articles.php/1678/
archbishops-presidential-address-13th-meeting-of-the-anglican-
consultative-council.

5. The Biblical Prohibitions

There are four main biblical passages which refer, or appear to refer to the question of same-sex activity negatively:

1. the story of Sodom (Genesis 19:1-13), with which it is natural to associate the very similar story of Gibeah (Judges 19);

2. the Levitical texts (Leviticus 18:22; 20:13) which explicitly prohibit having "sexual relations with a man as one does with a woman";

3. the apostle Paul's portrayal of decadent pagan society in his day (Romans 1:18-32); and

4. two Pauline lists of sinners, each of which includes a reference to homosexual practice of some kind (1 Corinthians 6:9-10; 1 Timothy 1:8-11).

1. The stories of Sodom and Gibeah

The Genesis narrative makes it clear that "the people of Sodom were wicked and were sinning greatly against the LORD"

(Genesis 13:13), and that "the outcry against Sodom and Gomorrah" was "so great and their sin so grievous" that God determined to investigate it (Genesis 18:20-21) and in the end "overthrew those cities and the entire plain, destroying all those living in the cities" (Genesis 19:25) by an act of judgment which was entirely consistent with the justice of "the Judge of all the earth" (Genesis 18:25). There is no controversy about this background to the biblical story. The question is, what was the sin of the people of Sodom (and Gomorrah) which merited their obliteration? Many Christians have assumed that they were guilty of homosexual practice, which they attempted (unsuccessfully) to inflict on the two angels whom Lot was entertaining in his home.

But theologian Sherwin Bailey, in re-evaluating the evidence, challenged this interpretation on two main grounds, and it is important to consider his arguments. First, in his view, the phrase "Bring them out to us, that we may know them" (as the ESV renders it) need not necessarily mean "so that we can have sex with them" (Genesis 19:5). The Hebrew word for "know" (*yada*') occurs 943 times in the Old Testament, of which only ten occurrences refer to physical intercourse, and even then only to heterosexual intercourse. It would therefore be better to translate the phrase "so that we may get acquainted with them". We can then understand the men's violence as due to their anger that Lot had exceeded his rights as a resident alien, for he had welcomed two strangers into his home "whose intentions might be hostile and whose credentials had not been examined".[28] In this case the sin of

---

28 Derrick Sherwin Bailey, *Homosexuality and the Western Christian Tradition* (London: Longmans, Green, 1955), p. 4.

Sodom was to invade the privacy of Lot's home and flout the ancient rules of hospitality. Lot begged them to desist because, he said, the two men "have come under the protection of my roof" (v 8).

However, Robert Gagnon, in what must be the most comprehensive and encyclopaedic treatise on the Bible and homosexuality, entitled *The Bible and Homosexual Practice: Texts and Hermeneutics*, comments that though hospitality may be part of the story, the focus of it is on the demeaning and dehumanising act of homosexual rape. Commenting on the sins of Sodom, he says of homosexual intercourse itself that it treated a man "as though his masculine identity counted for nothing, as though he were not a man but a woman. To penetrate another man was to treat him like an *assinnu*, like someone whose 'masculinity had been transformed into femininity'. Thus three elements (attempted penetration of males, attempted rape, inhospitality) and perhaps a fourth (unwitting, attempted sex with angels) combined to make this a particularly egregious example of human depravity that justifies God's act of total destruction."[29]

Second, Bailey argued that the rest of the Old Testament nowhere suggests that the nature of Sodom's offence was homosexual. Instead, Isaiah implies that it was hypocrisy and social injustice, Jeremiah adultery, deceit and general wickedness, and Ezekiel arrogance, greed and indifference to the poor (Isaiah 1:10ff.; Jeremiah 23:14; Ezekiel 16:49ff.; cf. the references in the Apocrypha: to pride in Ecclesiasticus 16:8 and to inhospitality in Wisdom 19:8). Then Jesus himself

---

29 Robert A. J. Gagnon, *The Bible and Homosexual Practice: Texts and Hermeneutics* (Nashville: Abingdon Press, 2001), pp. 75-76.

(though Bailey does not mention this) on three separate occasions alluded to the inhabitants of Sodom and Gomorrah, declaring that it would be "more bearable" for them on the day of judgment than for those who reject his gospel (Matthew 10:15; 11:24; Luke 10:12). Yet in all these references there is not even a whiff or rumour of homosexual malpractice. It is only when we reach the Palestinian pseudepigraphical writings of the second century BC that Sodom's sin is identified as unnatural sexual behaviour.[30] This finds a clear echo in the letter of Jude, in which it is said that "Sodom and Gomorrah and the surrounding towns gave themselves up to sexual immorality and perversion" (v 7), and in the works of Philo and Josephus, Jewish writers who were shocked by the homosexual practices of Greek society.

Sherwin Bailey handled the Gibeah story in the same way, for they are closely parallel. Another resident alien (this time an anonymous "old man") invites two strangers (not angels, but a Levite and his concubine) into his home. Evil men surround the house and make the same demand as the Sodomites, that the visitor be brought out "so that we can have sex with him". The owner of the house first begs them not to be so "vile" to his "guest", and then offers his daughter and the concubine to them instead. The sin of the men of Gibeah, it is again suggested, was not their proposal of homosexual intercourse but their violation of the laws of hospitality.

---

30 Sherwin Bailey gives references in the Book of Jubilees and the Testaments of the Twelve Patriarchs, in *Homosexuality and the Western Christian Tradition*, pp. 11–20. There is an even fuller evaluation of the writings of the intertestamental period in Peter Coleman, *Christian Attitudes to Homosexuality* (London: SPCK, 1980), pp. 58–85.

Although Bailey must have known that his reconstruction of both stories was at most tentative, he yet made the exaggerated claim that "there is not the least reason to believe, as a matter of either historical fact or of revealed truth, that the city of Sodom and its neighbours were destroyed because of their homosexual practices."[31] Instead, the Christian tradition about same-sex activity was derived from late, apocryphal Jewish sources.

But Sherwin Bailey's case is not convincing for a number of reasons:

- *The adjectives "wicked", "vile" and "outrageous" (Genesis 19:7; Judges 19:23) do not seem appropriate to describe a breach of hospitality.*
- *The offer of women instead, equally reprehensible as it is, "does look as if there is some sexual connotation to the episode."[32]*
- *Although the verb yada is used only ten times of sexual intercourse, Bailey omits to mention that six of these occurrences are in Genesis and one is in the Sodom story itself (about Lot's daughters, who had not "known" a man, v 8).*
- *For those of us who take the New Testament documents seriously, Jude's unequivocal reference to the "sexual immorality and perversion" of Sodom and Gomorrah (v 7) cannot be dismissed as merely an error copied from Jewish pseudepigrapha.*

To be sure, homosexual behaviour was not Sodom's only sin, but according to Scripture it was certainly one of its sins, which brought down upon it the fearful judgment of God.[33]

---

31 Bailey, Ibid., p. 27.

32 See James D. Martin, in Macourt (ed.), *Towards a Theology of Gay Liberation*, p. 53.

33 **Editor's note:** *I have not amended or removed this section, as it is part of John Stott's original argument. However, this is one of the*

John Stott

2. The Leviticus texts

Both texts in Leviticus belong to the "Holiness Code", which is the heart of the book and which challenges the people of God to follow his laws and not copy the practices either of Egypt (where they used to live) or of Canaan (to which he was bringing them). These practices included sexual relations within the prohibited degrees, a variety of sexual deviations, child sacrifice, idolatry and social injustice of different kinds. It is in this context that we must read the following two texts:

> Do not have sexual relations with a man as one does with a woman; that is detestable. (Leviticus 18:22)

> If a man has sexual relations with a man as one does with a woman, both of them have done what is detestable. They are to be put to death; their blood will be on their own heads. (Leviticus 20:13)

"It is hardly open to doubt," wrote Bailey, "that both the laws in Leviticus relate to ordinary homosexual acts between men, and not to ritual or other acts performed in the name of religion."[34] Others, however, think differently. They point out that the two texts are embedded in a context preoccupied largely with ritual cleanness, and Peter Coleman adds that the word translated "detestable" or "abomination" in both verses is associated with idolatry: "In English the word expresses

---

rare points at which I find his argument at least partly unpersuasive. While there is certainly a sexual element to Sodom's sin, the fact that the sexual activity intended by the men of Sodom would not be consensual means that it is not legitimate to apply the Bible's condemnation of it to consensual same-sex activity.

34 Bailey, *Homosexuality and the Western Christian Tradition*, p. 30.

disgust or disapproval, but in the Bible its predominant meaning is concerned with religious truth rather than morality or aesthetics".[35]

Are these prohibitions merely religious taboos, then? Are they connected with that other prohibition, "No Israelite man or woman is to become a shrine-prostitute" (Deuteronomy 23:17)? Certainly the Canaanite fertility cult did include ritual prostitution, and therefore provided both male and female "shrine-prostitutes" (although there is no clear evidence that either engaged in homosexual intercourse). The evil kings of Israel and Judah were constantly introducing them into the religion of Yahweh, and the righteous kings were constantly expelling them (see, for example, 1 Kings 14:22ff.; 15:12; 22:46; 2 Kings 23:7).

One could argue, therefore, that the Levitical texts prohibit religious practices which have long since ceased, and have no relevance to same-sex partnerships today. The burden of proof would be with such an argument, however. As William J. Webb points out in his recent work on hermeneutics, the issue here is primarily one of sexual boundaries.[36] The incest laws protect the boundary between parent and child; the bestiality laws protect the boundary between human and animal. Similarly, these homosexual boundaries prohibit intercourse between members of the same sex. They are not culturally determined boundaries in that they change as Scripture develops, but transcultural, prohibiting such activities in any place at any time.

---

35 Coleman, *Christian Attitudes to Homosexuality*, p. 49.

36 William J. Webb, *Slaves, Women and Homosexuals: Exploring the Hermeneutics of Cultural Analysis* (Downers Grove: InterVarsity, 2001), pp. 250-51.

So the plain, natural interpretation of these two verses is that they prohibit homosexual intercourse of every kind. The requirement of the death penalty (long since abrogated, of course) indicates the extreme seriousness with which homosexual practices were viewed.

3. Paul's teaching in Romans 1

> Because of this, God gave them over to shameful lusts. Even their women exchanged natural sexual relations for unnatural ones. In the same way the men also abandoned natural relations with women and were inflamed with lust for one another. Men committed shameful acts with other men, and received in themselves the due penalty for their error. (Romans 1:26-27)

All are agreed that the apostle is describing idolatrous pagans in the Graeco-Roman world of his day. They had a certain knowledge of God through the created universe (vv 19-20) and their own moral sense (v 32), yet they suppressed the truth they knew in order to practise wickedness. Instead of giving to God the honour due to him, they turned to idols, confusing the Creator with his creatures. In judgment upon them, "God gave them over" to their depraved mind and their decadent practices (vv 24, 26, 28), including "unnatural" sex.

So the passage seems at first sight to be a definite condemnation of homosexual behaviour. But two arguments are advanced on the other side. First, it is argued, Paul cannot be talking of people of homosexual orientation, since he says that their homosexual acts were "unnatural" and that they had previously had sex with women. But people of homosexual orientation would neither have had sex with the opposite sex, nor would homosexual sex be "unnatural" to them. Second, since Paul is evidently portraying the reckless and promiscuous behaviour of people whom God has judicially "given up", what relevance has this to committed, loving homosexual partnerships? These two arguments can be rebutted, however, especially by the apostle's reference to "nature"; that is, the created order, as I hope to show later.

Editor's note: *This conclusion has been upheld more recently by New Testament scholar E. P. Sanders in a major study of Paul and his writings. While Sanders himself explicitly supports what he describes as "the liberal attitude towards homosexuals", he does not think his own view is served by pretending that Paul thought other than he did: "We should let Paul say what he said, and then make the decisions that we should make, which should take into account the modern world."[37] So, with respect to Romans 1 he concludes, "Paul's own view of homosexual activities in Romans 1, where both males and females who have homosexual intercourse are condemned ... is a completely unambiguous condemnation of all homosexual activity."[38]*

---

37 E. P. Sanders, *Paul: The Apostle's Life, Letters and Thought.* (Fortress, Minneapolis, 2015), p. 370.

38 Ibid., p. 373.

4. The other Pauline texts

Do you not know that wrongdoers will not inherit the
kingdom of God? Do not be deceived: neither the sexually
immoral nor idolaters nor adulterers nor men who have
sex with men [*malakoi* and *arsenokoitai*] nor thieves nor
the greedy nor drunkards nor slanderers nor swindlers will
inherit the kingdom of God. (1 Corinthians 6:9–10)

We also know that the law is made not for the righteous
but for lawbreakers and rebels, the ungodly and sinful, the
unholy and irreligious, for those who kill their fathers or
mothers, for murderers, for the sexually immoral, for those
practising homosexuality [arsenokoitai], for slave traders
and liars and perjurers—and for whatever else is contrary to
the sound doctrine that conforms to the gospel concerning
the glory of the blessed God. (1 Timothy 1:9-10)

Here are two ugly lists of sins which Paul affirms to be
incompatible in the first place with the kingdom of God and
in the second place with either the law or the gospel. It will be
observed that one group of offenders are called *malakoi* and the
other (in both lists) *arsenokoitai*. What do these words mean?
The point is that all ten categories listed in 1 Corinthians 6:9-
10 (with the possible exception of "the greedy") denote people
who have offended by their actions—for example, idolaters,
adulterers and thieves.

The two Greek words *malakoi* and *arsenokoitai* should not
be combined, however, since they "have precise meanings. The
first is literally 'soft to the touch' and metaphorically, among
the Greeks, meant males (not necessarily boys) who played

the passive role in homosexual intercourse. The second means literally 'male in a bed', and the Greeks used this expression to describe the one who took the active role."[39]

Robert Gagnon translates *malakoi* as "the soft ones" and *arsenokoitai* as "males who take other males to bed".[40] Strikingly, the Septuagint, the Greek translation of the Old Testament, in Leviticus 20:13 includes the phrase *arsenos koitēn*, so this may well be the origin of the term, which does not appear elsewhere.[41] Peter Coleman suggests that "probably Paul had commercial pederasty in mind between older men and post-pubertal boys, the most common pattern of homosexual behaviour in the classical world."[42] If this is so, then once again it can be (and has been) argued that the Pauline condemnations are not relevant to homosexual adults who are both consenting and committed to one another. This is not, however, the conclusion which Peter Coleman himself draws. His summary is as follows:

> Taken together, St Paul's writings repudiate homosexual behaviour as a vice of the Gentiles in Romans, as a bar to the Kingdom in Corinthians, and as an offence to be repudiated by the moral law in 1 Timothy.[43]

Reviewing these biblical references to homosexual behaviour,

---

39 Coleman, *Christian Attitudes to Homosexuality*, pp. 95-96.

40 Gagnon, *The Bible and Homosexual Practice*, p. 306.

41 **Editor's note:** More recently, E. P. Sanders has also supported this interpretation. See *Paul: The Apostle's Life, Letters and Thought*, pp. 366-8.

42 Coleman, *Christian Attitudes to Homosexuality*, p. 277.

43 Ibid., p. 101.

which I have grouped, we have to agree that there are only a handful of them. Must we then conclude that the topic is marginal to the main thrust of the Bible? Must we further concede that they constitute a rather flimsy basis on which to take a firm stand against a homosexual lifestyle? Are they right who claim that the biblical prohibitions are "highly specific"[44] —against violations of hospitality (Sodom and Gibeah), against cultic taboos (Leviticus), against shameless orgies (Romans) and against male prostitution or the corruption of the young (1 Corinthians and 1 Timothy), and that none of these passages allude to, let alone condemn, a loving partnership between people of homosexual orientation?

Plausible as it may sound, we cannot handle the biblical material in this way. The Christian rejection of homosexual practices does not rest on "a few isolated and obscure proof texts" (as is sometimes said), whose traditional explanation (it is further claimed) can be overthrown. The negative prohibitions of homosexual practices in Scripture make sense only in the light of its positive teaching in Genesis 1 and 2 about human sexuality and heterosexual marriage.[45] Yet without the wholesome positive teaching of the Bible on sex and marriage, our perspective on the homosexual question is bound to be skewed.

---

44 Rictor Norton, in Macourt (ed.), *Towards a Theology of Gay Liberation*, p. 58.

45 Sherwin Bailey's book contains no allusion to these chapters at all. And even Peter Coleman, whose *Christian Attitudes to Homosexuality* is comprehensive, mentions them only in a passing reference to 1 Corinthians 6, where Paul quotes Genesis 2:24.

6. Contemporary Arguments Considered

Some Christians are not, however, satisfied with this biblical teaching about human sexuality and the institution of opposite-sex marriage. They bring forward a number of objections to it, in order to defend the legitimacy of same-sex sexual partnerships.

The argument about Scripture and culture

Traditionally, it has been assumed that the Bible condemns all same-sex activity. But are the biblical writers reliable guides in this matter? Were their horizons not bounded by their own experience and culture? The cultural argument usually takes one of two forms. Firstly, the biblical authors were addressing themselves to questions relevant to their own circumstances, but these were very different from ours. In the Sodom and Gibeah stories they were preoccupied either with conventions of hospitality in the ancient Near East which are now obsolete or (if the sin was sexual at all) with the phenomenon of gang rape. In the Levitical laws the concern was with antiquated fertility rituals, while Paul was addressing himself to the particular sexual preferences of Greek pederasts. It is all so antiquarian. The biblical authors' imprisonment in their own cultures renders their teaching on this topic irrelevant.

The second and complementary culture problem is that the biblical writers were not addressing themselves to our questions. Thus the problem of Scripture is not only with its teaching but also with its silence. Paul (let alone the Old Testament authors) knew nothing of post-Freudian psychology. They had never heard of "homosexual orientation"; they knew only about certain practices. The very notion that two men or two women could fall in love with each other and develop a deeply loving, stable relationship comparable or equivalent to marriage simply never entered their heads.[46]

If the only biblical teaching on this topic were to be found in the prohibition texts, it might be difficult to answer these objections. But once those texts are seen in relation to the divine institution of marriage, we are in possession of a principle of divine revelation which is universally applicable. It was applicable to the cultural situations of both the ancient Near East and the first-century Graeco-Roman world, and it is equally applicable to modern sexual questions of which the ancients were quite ignorant. The reason for the biblical prohibitions is the same reason why modern loving same-sex

---

46 **Editor's note:** *This is actually disputable. There were indeed consensual sexual relationships between adult males in the ancient world. For a very brief summary of the evidence, see the article by Peter Ould here: http://www.livingout.org/surely-the-homosexual-activity-prohibited-by-the-bible-was-totally-different-to-what-we-re-familiar-with-today-*

sexual partnerships must also be ruled out: namely that they are incompatible with God's created order. And since that order (opposite-sex monogamy) was established by creation, not culture, its validity is both permanent and universal. There can be no "liberation" from God's created norms; true liberation is found only in accepting them.

This argumentation is the opposite of the "biblical literalism" of which we may be accused. It is rather to look beneath the surface of the biblical prohibitions to the essential positives of divine revelation on sexuality and marriage. It is significant that some who advocate same-sex partnerships omit Genesis 1 and 2 from their discussion, even though Jesus our Lord himself endorsed their teaching.

It is now important to look at gay relationships and their social context in a little more depth, and to consider the arguments used to support committed gay relationships.

The argument about creation and nature

People sometimes make this kind of statement: "I'm gay because God made me that way. So gay must be good. I cannot believe that God would create people homosexual and then deny them the right to sexual self-expression. I intend, therefore, to affirm, and indeed celebrate, what I am by creation." Or again, "You may say that homosexual practice is against nature and normality; but it's not against my nature, nor is it in the slightest degree abnormal for me." Norman Pittenger was quite outspoken in his use of this argument. A gay person, he wrote, is "not an 'abnormal' person with 'unnatural' desires and habits." On the contrary, "A heterosexually oriented person acts 'naturally' when he acts heterosexually, while a homosexually oriented person acts equally 'naturally' when he acts in accordance with his basic, inbuilt homosexual desire and drive."[47]

One might also argue that same-sex is "natural", (a) because in many primitive societies it is fairly acceptable, (b) because in some advanced civilisations (for example, ancient Greece) it was even idealised, and (c) because it is said to be quite widespread in animals.[48]

In any case, these arguments express an extremely subjective view of what is "natural" and "normal". We should not accept Norman Pittenger's statement that there are "no eternal standards of normality or naturalness".[49] Nor can we agree that animal behaviour sets standards for human behaviour! God has established a norm for sex and marriage by creation. This was already recognised in the Old Testament era. Thus sexual relations with an animal were forbidden, because "that is a perversion" (Leviticus 18:23); in other words a violation or confusion of nature, which indicates an "embryonic sense of natural law".[50]

The same verdict is passed on Sodom by the second-century-BC Testament of Naphtali: "As the sun and the stars do not change their order, so the tribe of Naphtali are to obey God rather than the disorderliness of idolatry. Recognising in

---

47 Norman Pittenger, *Time for Consent* (London: SCM, 1976), pp. 7, 73.

48 On the evidence that homosexuality is pervasive among animals, see Bruce Bagemihl, *Biological Exuberance: Animal Homosexuality and Natural Diversity* (New York: St Martin's Press, 1999), and more recently Aldo Poiani, *Animal Homosexuality: A Biosocial Perspective* (Cambridge: Cambridge University Press, 2010).

49 Pittenger, *Time for Consent*, p. 7.

50 Coleman, *Christian Attitudes to Homosexuality*, p. 50.

all created things the Lord who made them, they are not to become as Sodom, which changed the order of nature..."[51]

The same concept was clearly in Paul's mind in Romans 1. When he wrote of women who had "exchanged natural sexual relations for unnatural ones", and of men who had "abandoned natural relations", he meant by "nature" (*physis*) the natural order of things which God has established (as in Romans 2:14 and 11:24). What Paul was condemning, therefore, was not the perverted behaviour of heterosexual people who were acting against their nature, as John Boswell argued, but any human behaviour that is against "nature"—that is, against God's created order.[52] Richard B. Hays has written a thorough rebuttal of John Boswell's exegesis of Romans 1. He provides ample contemporary evidence that the opposition of "natural" (*kata physin*) and "unnatural" (*para physin*) was "very frequently used ... as a way of distinguishing between heterosexual and homosexual behaviour".[53]

Other commentators on Romans 1 confirm his conclusion. As C. K. Barrett puts it, "In the obscene pleasures to which he [Paul] refers is to be seen precisely that perversion of the created order which may be expected when men put the creation in place of the Creator".[54] Similarly, Charles Cranfield

---

51 Quoted by Coleman, Ibid., p. 71, chapter 3.3–5.

52 John Boswell, *Christianity, Social Tolerance and Homosexuality* (Chicago: University of Chicago Press, 1981), pp. 107ff.

53 Richard B. Hays, "A Response to John Boswell's Exegesis of Romans 1", *Journal of Religious Ethics*, Spring 1986, p. 192. See also his *The Moral Vision of the New Testament* (Edinburgh: T. & T. Clark, 1996), pp. 383–89.

54 C. K. Barrett, *Commentary on the Epistle to the Romans* (London: A. & C. Black, 1962), p. 39.

writes that by "natural" and "unnatural", "Paul clearly means 'in accordance with the intention of the Creator' and 'contrary to the intention of the Creator', respectively."

Again, "the decisive factor in Paul's use of it [*physis*, "nature"] is his biblical doctrine of creation. It denotes that order which is manifest in God's creation and which men have no excuse for failing to recognise and respect."[55] Robert Gagnon states that "same-sex intercourse is 'beyond' or 'in excess of' nature in the sense that it transgresses the boundaries for sexuality both established by God and transparent in nature even to Gentiles".[56]

Editor's note: *This conclusion is actually shared by William Loader, a New Testament scholar who wants the church to affirm same-sex relationships, but is honest enough to admit that support for such a view cannot be found in Paul. As he puts it in his major study on sexuality and the New Testament, commenting on Romans 1:*

"Paul employs same-sex passion and its fulfilment in same-sex intercourse, among both women and men, as his first item of evidence for human depravity. ... I will therefore want to take what Paul says seriously, but his views are to be assessed in the light of all relevant available information, as a result of which we should feel free to

---

55 C. E. B. Cranfield, "Commentary on Romans", in the *International Critical Commentary* (Edinburgh: T&T Clark, 1975), vol. 1, p. 126. He attributes the same meaning to *physis* in his comment on 1 Corinthians 11:14. What the NIV translates "the very nature of things" Professor Cranfield renders "the very way God has made us".

56 Gagnon, *The Bible and Homosexual Practice*, pp. 299–302.

reach different conclusions from Paul if the evidence suggests that this is appropriate." [57]

An appeal to the created order should also be our response to another argument. Some point out that the early church distinguished between primary and secondary issues, insisting on agreement about the former but allowing freedom to disagree about the latter. The two examples of Christian liberty which they usually quote are circumcision and idol-meats. They then draw a parallel with homosexual practice, suggesting that it is a second-order issue in which we can give one another freedom. But actually the early church was more subtle than that. The Jerusalem Council (Acts 15) decreed that circumcision was definitely not necessary for salvation (a first-order question), but allowed its continuance as a matter of policy or culture (second-order). The Council also decided that, although of course idolatry was forbidden (first-order), eating idol-meats was not necessarily idolatrous, so that Christians with a strong, educated conscience might eat them (second-order). Thus the second-order issues, in which Christian liberty was allowed, were neither theological nor moral but cultural. This is not the case with homosexual practice.

A second parallel is sometimes drawn. When the debate over women's ordination was at its height, General Synod agreed that the Church should not be obliged to choose between the two positions (for and against), declaring one to be right and the other wrong, but should rather preserve unity

---

57 William Loader, *The New Testament on Sexuality* (Grand Rapids: Eerdmans, 2012), pp. 320-1.

by recognising both to have integrity. In consequence, we are living with "the two integrities". Why, it is asked, should we not equally acknowledge "two integrities" in relation to same-sex partnerships, and not force people to choose? The answer should be clear. Even if women's ordination is a second-order issue (which not all would accept in any case), homosexual partnerships are not. Gender in relation to marriage is a much more fundamental matter than gender in relation to ministry. Marriage has been recognized as an opposite-sex union from the beginning of God's creation and institution; it is basic to human society as God intended it, and its biblical basis is incontrovertible. As Wolfhart Pannenberg, Professor of Theology at Munich University, puts it, "The biblical assessments of homosexual practice are unambiguous in their rejection." He therefore concludes that a church which were to recognise same-sex unions as equivalent to marriage "would cease to be the one, holy, catholic and apostolic church."[58]

The argument about quality of relationships

Another common argument in favour of same-sex sexual relationships borrows from Scripture the truth that love is the greatest thing in the world (which it is), and from the "new morality" or "situation ethics" of the 1960s the notion that love is an adequate criterion by which to judge every relationship (which it is not). Yet this view is gaining ground today.

One of the first official documents to embrace it was the Friends' Report "Towards a Quaker View of Sex" (1963). It included the statements, "One should no more deplore

---

58 *Christianity Today*, 11 November 1996. Available online at http://www.christianitytoday.com/ct/1996/november11/6td035.html.

'homosexuality' than left-handedness," and, "Surely it is the nature and quality of a relationship that matters".[59] Similarly, in 1979 the Methodist Church's Division of Social Responsibility, in its report "A Christian Understanding of Human Sexuality", argued that "homosexual activities" are "not intrinsically wrong", since "the quality of any homosexual relationship is … to be assessed by the same basic criteria which have been applied to heterosexual relationships. For homosexual men and women, permanent relationships characterized by love can be an appropriate Christian way of expressing their sexuality."[60]

The same year (1979) an Anglican working party issued the report "Homosexual Relationships: A Contribution to Discussion". It was more cautious, judicious and ambivalent than the Quaker and Methodist reports. Its authors did not feel able to repudiate centuries of Christian tradition, yet they "did not think it possible to deny" that in some circumstances individuals may "justifiably choose" a homosexual relationship in their search for companionship and sexual love, "similar" to those found in marriage.[61] Surely any relationship characterised by mutual commitment, affection, faithfulness and support should be affirmed as good, not rejected as evil? It rescues people from loneliness, selfishness and promiscuity, and it can be just as rich and responsible, as liberating and fulfilling, as an opposite-sex marriage.[62]

---

59 The Friends' Report, "Towards a Quaker View of Sex" (1963), p. 21 and p. 36.

60 Methodist Church's Division of Social Responsibility, "A Christian Understanding of Human Sexuality" (1979), chapter 9.

61 See chapter 5 of the report.

62 *Editor's note: The same argument is also evident in the Pilling report.*

In the spring of 1997, in a lecture delivered at St Martin-in-the-Fields in London, Bishop John Austin Baker gave his own version of this argument. Formerly Bishop of Salisbury, he had chaired the Church of England's Doctrine Commission, as well as the drafting group which in 1991 produced the report "Issues in Human Sexuality", which argued that while same-sex relationships could be permitted among the laity without church discipline, they were not appropriate for clergy, who were expected to live out the teaching of the church. In his lecture, he astonished the church by his apparent *volte-face*. The goal of Christian discipleship, he rightly affirmed, is "Christ-likeness"—that is, "a creative living out of the values, priorities and attitudes that marked his humanity", especially of love. Now sex in marriage can be "a true making of love", and "erotic love can and often does have the same beneficial effects in the life of same-sex couples".

However, the argument based on the quality of same-sex love is flawed.

Love needs the law

While it is of course true that love is the only moral absolute, even love needs law to guide it. Not in the sense of keeping the Old Testament law in order to be saved, or in terms of observing the various requirements of the Torah which have been fulfilled in Christ. But for Christians, the moral Law has not been abolished. In emphasising love for God and neighbour as the two greatest commandments, Jesus and his apostles did not discard all the others. Indeed, the rest of the Law and the Prophets "hang" (NIV) or "depend" (ESV) on the commands to love God and neighbour (Matthew 22:40).

All the other moral commands flow out from and express the commands to love God and our neighbour. They spell out more specifically how we are to love our neighbours as ourselves. Or, as Paul puts it, love "sums up" and "fulfils" the Law (Romans 13:8 and 10 and Galatians 5:14). Love and Law cannot be separated. Indeed, Jesus said, "If you love me, keep my command (John 14:15)."

So then, although the loving quality of a relationship is an essential criterion, it is not by itself a sufficient criterion to authenticate such a relationship. Let me give you an illustration, drawn from my own pastoral experience. On several different occasions a married man has told me that he has fallen in love with another woman. When I have gently remonstrated with him, he has responded in words like these: "Yes, I agree, I already have a wife and family. But this new relationship is the real thing. We were made for each other. Our love for each other has a quality and depth we have never known before. It must be right." But no, I have had to say to him, it is not right. No man is justified in breaking his marriage covenant with his wife on the ground that the quality of his love for another woman is richer. Quality of love is not the only yardstick by which to measure what is good or right.

Similarly, we should not deny that homosexual relationships can be loving. But the love quality of same-sex sexual relationships is not sufficient to justify them. Indeed, I have to add that in a sense they are incompatible with true love, because they are incompatible with God's law. Love is concerned for the highest welfare of the beloved. And our highest human welfare is found in obedience to God's law and purpose, not in revolt against them.

The argument about justice and rights

If some argue for homosexual partnerships on the basis of the love involved, others do so on the basis of justice. Desmond Tutu, for example, formerly Archbishop of Cape Town and universally admired for his courageous stand against apartheid and for racial equality, has several times said that for him the homosexual question is a simple matter of justice. Others agree. The justice argument runs like this: "Just as we may not discriminate between persons on account of their gender, colour, ethnicity or class, so we may not discriminate between persons on account of their sexual preference. For the God of the Bible is the God of justice, who is described as loving justice and hating injustice. Therefore the quest for justice must be a paramount obligation of the people of God. Now that slaves, women and ethnic minorities have been liberated, gay liberation is long overdue. What civil rights activists were in the 1950s and 60s, gay-rights activists are today. We should support them in their cause and join them in their struggle."

The vocabulary of oppression, liberation, rights and justice, however, needs careful definition. Gay liberation presupposes an oppression from which homosexual people need to be set free, and gay rights imply that homosexual people are suffering a wrong which should be righted. But what is this oppression, this wrong, this injustice? Where they are being despised and mistreated by sections of society on account of their sexual orientation, and are in fact victims of homophobia, then indeed they have a grievance which must be redressed. God opposes such discrimination and requires us to love and respect all human beings without distinction. If, on the other hand, the "wrong" or "injustice" complained of is the church's refusal to recognise homosexual partnerships as a legitimate alternative to heterosexual marriages, then talk of "justice" is inappropriate, since human beings may not claim as a "right" what God has not given them.

The analogy between slavery, racism, the oppression of women and homosexuality is inexact and misleading. In each case we need to clarify the Creator's original intention. Thus, in spite of misguided attempts to justify slavery and racism from Scripture, both are fundamentally incompatible with the created equality of human beings. Similarly, the Bible honours womanhood by affirming that men and women share equally in the image of God and the stewardship of the environment, and any teaching on masculine "headship" or responsibility may not be interpreted as contradicting this equality. But sexual intercourse belongs, according to the plain teaching of Scripture, to marriage between a man and a woman alone. Therefore, homosexual intercourse cannot be regarded as a permissible equivalent, let alone a divine right. True gay liberation (like all authentic liberation) is not freedom from God's revealed purpose in order to construct our own morality; it is, rather, freedom from our self-willed rebellion in order to love and obey him.

The argument about acceptance and the gospel

"Surely," some people are saying, "it is the duty of Christians to accept everybody. Paul told us to accept—indeed welcome— one another. If God has welcomed somebody, who are we to pass judgment on them (Romans 14:1ff.; 15:7)?" Norman Pittenger says, "The whole point of the Christian gospel is that God loves and accepts us just as we are".[63] This is a very confused statement of the gospel, however. God does indeed accept us "just as we are", and we do not have to make ourselves good first; indeed we cannot. But his "acceptance" means that he fully and freely forgives all who repent and believe, not that he condones our continuance in sin. Again, it is true that we are called to accept one another, but as fellow penitents and fellow pilgrims, not as fellow sinners who are resolved to persist in our sinning. Michael Vasey makes much of the fact that Jesus was called (and was) "the friend of sinners". His offer of friendship to sinners like us is truly wonderful. But he welcomes us in order to redeem and transform us, not to leave us alone in our sins. No acceptance, either by God or by the church, is promised to us if we harden our hearts against God's word and will—only judgement.

63 Pittenger, *Time for Consent*

REAL LIVES
Graham's story

I had the enormous privilege of growing up in a loving church and always being aware of the goodness of God. Alongside that, however, I wrestled with a growing awareness of same-sex attraction. I first spoke of my feelings to another Christian at the age of 16, and 16 years later those feelings have not gone away; but neither has the deep conviction that walking with Jesus is incompatible with homosexual relationships.

I empathise fully with those who speak of the pain caused by the church's teaching on this subject—but there is a side to this story that is often unheard. I and many like me feel a deep sadness when our walk with Christ, and our choice to deny ourselves a same-sex relationship, are so often depicted as fuelled by bigotry or an outdated reading of the Bible.

I have heard many passionate arguments that we must change our teaching on sexuality because not all facing this temptation seem able to bear the struggle; this view is presented as a change grounded in pastoral wisdom and love. My experience has been the absolute reverse. I have chosen a path of abstention from homosexual practice, but not as the result of some special strength or ability on my part, but because the Bible's teaching is inescapably clear. The walk has not been easy. I have known periods of intense anguish and anger, but I have also experienced the mighty and compassionate hand of God pulling me free from that. That has been a wonderful gift, and an experience that resonates with the teaching of Jesus and the New Testament about the experience of living for him.

Jesus tells us that we must take up our cross daily (Luke 9:23); Paul urges us to offer our bodies as living sacrifices (Romans 12:1); James says we must consider it pure joy when we face trials of many kinds (James 1:2). There is no shortage of evidence that the genuine path of following Christ is "narrow" and unpopular; and yet we tread that path because Jesus promises that it will lead to life—it's worth it (Matthew 7:13-14). A faithful response to God and his word, and to those struggling in my situation, would be to stand with us as we seek to honour Christ with our sexuality. He works in our weakness and honours us as we stand together as his family, and there is so much we may learn from supporting each other in our different struggles.

It is my conviction that changing our teaching to accommodate homosexual relationships does not just undermine a handful of Bible verses, but compromises the whole vision of the gospel. Jesus is worth everything. Jesus is able to keep us from falling. I fear we are accepting a message that says the single life is unbearable and life is not possible without sex. That is a lie. These views have no support in Scripture, or the wonderful life of Christ, which we are called to imitate. Dare we ever say that anything is too much to offer to God? We may groan with creation, (Romans 8), as we await his return—but what a reward awaits us: "Everyone who has left houses or brothers or sisters or father or mother or wife or children or fields for my sake will receive a hundred times as much and will receive eternal life" (Matthew 19:29). And what joy Jesus brings us as he walks with us and cheers us on the way.

7. Faith, Hope and Love

If homosexual practice must be regarded, in the light of the whole biblical revelation, not as a variant within the wide range of accepted normality, but as a deviation from God's norm, and if we should therefore call gay and lesbian people to abstain from same-sex practices and partnerships, what advice and help can we give to encourage them to respond to this call? I would like to finish by taking Paul's triad of faith, hope and love, and applying it to this particular question.

The Christian call to faith

Faith is our human response to divine revelation: it is believing God's word.

First, faith accepts God's standards. The only alternative to opposite-sex marriage is singleness and sexual abstinence. I think I know the implications of this. Nothing has helped me to understand the pain of homosexual celibacy more than Alex Davidson's moving book *The Returns of Love*.[64]

The secular world says, "Sex is essential to human fulfilment. To expect homosexual people to abstain from sexual intimacy is to condemn them to frustration and to drive them to neurosis, despair and even suicide. It's outrageous to ask them to deny themselves what to them is a normal and natural mode of sexual expression. It's 'inhuman and inhumane'.[65] Indeed, it's positively cruel."

But no, the teaching of the Word of God is different. Sexual experience is not essential to human fulfilment. To be sure, it is a good gift of God, but it is not given to all, and it is not indispensable to humanness. People were saying in Paul's day that it was. Their approach was, "Food for the stomach and the stomach for food"; sex for the body and the body for sex (see 1 Corinthians 6:13). But this is a lie of the devil. Jesus Christ was single, yet perfect in his humanity. So it is possible to be single and human at the same time! Besides, God's commands are good and not grievous. The yoke of Christ brings rest, not turmoil; conflict comes only to those who resist it.

At the very centre of Christian discipleship is our participation in the death and resurrection of Jesus Christ. The St Andrew's Day Statement on this subject (1995), commissioned by the Church of England Evangelical Council, emphasised this. We are "called to follow in the way of the cross", for "we all are summoned to various forms of self-denial. The struggle against disordered desires, or the misdirection of

---

64 Alex Davidson, *The Returns of Love* (London: InterVarsity Press, 1970).

65 Norman Pittenger, in Macourt (ed.), *Towards a Theology of Gay Liberation*, p. 87.

innocent desire, is part of every Christian's life, consciously undertaken in baptism." But after struggle comes victory, out of death resurrection.[66]

So ultimately it is a crisis of faith: whom shall we believe? God or the world? Shall we submit to the lordship of Jesus, or succumb to the pressures of prevailing culture? The true "orientation" that matters is not our sexual orientation, but whether we are oriented towards trusting in God, and obeying his will.

---

66 The St Andrew's Day Statement (published 30 November 1995) begins with three theological "Principles" relating to the incarnate Lord (in whom we come to know both God and ourselves), the Holy Spirit (who enables us to interpret the times), and God the Father (who restores the broken creation in Christ). The statement's second half consists of three "Applications" relating to such questions as our human identity, empirical observations, the reaffirmation of the good news of salvation and the hope of final fulfilment in Christ. Two years later, *The Way Forward?* was published, with the subtitle "Christian voices on homosexuality and the church". This symposium, edited by Tim Bradshaw, consists of thirteen responses to the St Andrew's Day Statement, from a wide range of different viewpoints. One appreciates the call to patient and serious theological reflection. But it is inaccurate to write of "dialogue" and "diatribe" as if they were the only options. Some of us have been listening and reflecting for thirty or forty years! How long must the process continue before we are allowed to reach a conclusion? In spite of claims to the contrary, no fresh evidence has been produced which could overthrow the clear witness of Scripture and the long-standing tradition of the church. The St Andrew's Day Statement says that the church recognises two vocations (marriage and singleness), and adds that "there is no place for the Church to confer legitimacy upon alternatives to these". Further, the authors of the statement do not consider that "the considerable burden of proof to support a major change in the Church's teaching and practice has been met" by the contributors to the book (p. 3). Yet the book makes a more uncertain sound than the statement. So by all means let there be serious theological reflection, but then let the church make up its mind.

Second, faith accepts God's grace. Abstinence is not only good, if God calls us to celibacy; it is also possible. Many deny it, however. "You know the imperious strength of our sex drive," they say. "To ask us to control ourselves is just not on." It is "so near to an impossibility," writes Norman Pittenger, "that it's hardly worth talking about".[67]

Really? What, then, are we to make of Paul's statement following his warning to the Corinthians that "men who have sex with men" will not inherit God's kingdom? "And that is what some of you were," he cries. "But you were washed, you were sanctified, you were justified in the name of the Lord Jesus Christ and by the Spirit of our God" (1 Corinthians 6:11). And what shall we say to the millions of heterosexual people who are single? To be sure, all unmarried people experience the pain of struggle and loneliness. But how can we call ourselves Christians and declare that chastity is impossible? It is made harder by the sexual obsession of contemporary society. And we make it harder for ourselves if we listen to the world's plausible arguments, or lapse into self-pity, or feed our imagination with pornographic material and so inhabit a fantasy world in which Christ is not Lord, or ignore his command about plucking out our eyes and cutting off our hands and feet—that is, being ruthless with the avenues of temptation. But, whatever our "thorn in the flesh" may be, Christ comes to us as he came to Paul and says, "My grace is sufficient for you, for my power is made perfect in weakness"

67 Pittenger, *Time for Consent*, p. 7. Compare *The Courage to be Chaste: An Uncompromising Call to the Biblical Standard of Chastity* (New York: Paulist Press, 1986). Written by Benedict J. Groeschel, a Capuchin friar, the book contains much practical advice.

(2 Corinthians 12:9). To deny this is to portray Christians as the helpless victims of the world, the flesh and the devil, to demean them into being less than human, and to contradict the gospel of God's grace.

The Christian call to hope

I have said nothing so far about the possibility of change in sexual orientation for homosexual people. Our expectation of this possibility will depend largely on our understanding of the aetiology of the homosexual condition, and no final agreement on this has yet been reached. Many studies have been conducted, but they have failed to establish a single cause, whether inherited or learned. So scholars have tended to turn to theories of multiple causation, combining a biological predisposition (genetic and hormonal) with cultural and moral influences, and childhood environment and experience.[68]

Just as opinions differ on the causes of homosexuality, so they also differ on the possibilities and the means of change. This issue divides people into several categories. Some consider it unnecessary, some regard it as potentially harmful or damaging; some consider it possible; others consider it impossible.

---

68 **Editor's note:** For a recent and authoritative review article on this, see Eleanor Whiteway and Denis R Alexander, "Understanding the causes of same-sex attraction" in Science and Christian Belief (2015) 27, pp. 17-40, which concludes that "no one causal mechanism is both necessary and sufficient to explain the whole gamut of human sexual attraction. Sexual attraction is a highly complex trait, and it seems likely that across the variety of human sexes and cultures, different influences are more important at different times" (p. 40). Available online at https://www.scienceandchristianbelief.org/serve_pdf_free. php?filename=SCB+27-1+Whiteway+Alexander.pdf.

First, we have to recognise that the language of "cure" and "healing" is deeply shaming and dangerous. Secondly, there are many who regard the change of sexual orientation as impossible. "No known method ..." writes D. J. West, "offers hope of making any substantial reduction in the vast army of adults practising homosexuality". It would be "more realistic to find room for them in society". He pleads for "tolerance", though not for "encouragement", of homosexual behaviour.[69]

Are these views, however, not the despairing opinions of the secular mind? They challenge us to articulate a different position, which is to believe that at least some degree of change may take place in some people. Christians know that the homosexual orientation, being a deviation from God's norm, is not a sign of created order but of fallen disorder. How, then, can we acquiesce in it or declare it irreversible? We cannot, any more than we can acquiesce in the existence of lust towards someone of the opposite sex. But there is a question as to when and how we are to expect divine intervention and restoration to take place. The fact is that, though Christian claims of changes to sexual orientation are made, either through regeneration or through a subsequent work of the Holy Spirit, it is not easy to substantiate them.[70]

Martin Hallett, who before his conversion was active in the gay scene, has written a very honest account of his experience of what he calls "Christ's way out of homosexuality". He

---

69 D. J. West, *Homosexuality* (1955; 2nd ed., London: Pelican, 1960; 3rd ed., London: Duckworth, 1968), pp. 266, 273.

70 Nelson Gonzalez's article "Exploding Ex-Gay Myths", in *Regeneration Quarterly*, Vol. 1, no. 3, Summer 1995, challenged the aims and claims of the ex-gay movement.

is candid about his continuing vulnerability, his need for safeguards, his yearning for love and his occasional bouts of emotional turmoil. I am glad he entitled his autobiographical sketch *I Am Learning to Love* in the present tense, and subtitled it "A personal journey to wholeness in Christ". His final paragraph begins, "I have learnt; I am learning; I will learn to love God, other people and myself. This healing process will only be complete when I am with Jesus."[71]

True Freedom Trust has also published many testimonies in which homosexual Christian men and women bear witness to what Christ has done for them.[72] They have found a new identity in him, and have a new sense of personal fulfilment as children of God. They have been delivered from guilt, shame and fear by God's forgiving acceptance, and many have been set free from thraldom to their former sexual activity by the indwelling power of the Holy Spirit. But most have not experienced change in their sexual orientation, and, therefore, some inner pain continues alongside their new joy and peace. Here are two examples. "I would like to be able to end this story by saying that I no longer struggle with same-sex attraction, but this is not the case ... Maybe in the future he will change my desires and I will end up falling in love and getting married. On the other hand, maybe I am meant to live

---

71 Martin Hallett, *I Am Learning to Love* (Grand Rapids: Zondervan, 1987), p. 155. Martin Hallett founded the True Freedom Trust (TfT), which now offers an interdenominational "support and teaching ministry" for those who "experience same-sex attraction, but who choose not to embrace a gay identity or to pursue a same-sex relationship" and their families, friends and church leaders. They can be contacted through their website, www.truefreedomtrust.co.uk.

72 www.truefreedomtrust.co.uk/stories.

my life as a single man. Either way, I know he has an amazing plan for me and he will give me the strength for whatever I face!"[73] "The salvation of the cross has not removed my same-sex attractions. … [But] I can face every day through the joy given by God's grace and am empowered to live for him."[74]

Editor's note: *More recent research into attempts to bring a degree of change with respect to sexual orientation through psychotherapy has established two key findings. First, far from being harmful, such therapy helped to reduce the distress experienced by participants, even where they did not experience any change in their sexual orientation. Mark Yarhouse, a lead member of the team which carried out the research, comments that "participants tended to emphasise their relationship with God, their experience of God's love and acceptance, and spiritual growth".[75]*

Second, some people did indeed experience some reduction in their same-sex attractions—although without a "control" group it is impossible to demonstrate whether these changes were a result of the therapy or would have happened anyway.[76]

Is there really, then, no hope of a substantial change of inclination?

---

73 https://truefreedomtrust.co.uk/node/245.

74 https://truefreedomtrust.co.uk/node/226 and https://truefreedomtrust.co.uk/node/227.

75 Mark Yarhouse, *Homosexuality and the Christian.* (Bloomington, MN: Bethany House, 2010), p. 94.

76 See Stanton Jones and Mark A. Yarhouse, *Ex-Gays? A Longitudinal Study of Religiously Mediated Change in Sexual Orientation.* (Downers Grove, IL: IVP Academic, 2007).

The complete transformation of body, mind and spirit will not take place in this life. Some degree of disorder remains in all of us. But not for ever. The Christian's horizons are not bounded by this world. Jesus Christ is coming again; our bodies are going to be redeemed; sin, pain and death are going to be abolished; and both we and the universe are going to be transformed. Then we shall be finally liberated from everything which defiles or distorts us. This Christian assurance helps us to bear whatever our present pain may be. For pain there is, in the midst of peace. "We know that the whole creation has been groaning as in the pains of childbirth right up to the present time. Not only so, but we ourselves, who have the firstfruits of the Spirit, groan inwardly as we wait eagerly for our adoption to sonship, the redemption of our bodies" (Romans 8:22-23). Thus our groans express the birthpangs of the new age. We are convinced that "our present sufferings are not worth comparing with the glory that will be revealed in us" (Romans 8:18). This confident hope sustains us.

Alex Davidson derives comfort in the midst of his homosexuality from his Christian hope. "Isn't it one of the most wretched things about this condition," he writes, "that when you look ahead, the same impossible road seems to continue indefinitely? You're driven to rebellion when you think of there being no point in it and to despair when you think of there being no limit to it. That's why I find a comfort, when I feel desperate, or rebellious, or both, to remind myself of God's promise that one day it will be finished."[77]

---

77 Davidson, *The Returns of Love*, p. 51.

The Christian call to love

At present we are living "in between times", between the grace which we grasp by faith and the glory which we anticipate in hope. Between them lies love. Yet love is just what the church has generally failed to show to homosexual people. Jim Cotter complains bitterly about being treated as "objects of scorn and insult, of fear, prejudice and oppression".[78] Norman Pittenger describes the "vituperative" correspondence he has received, in which gay people are demeaned even by professing Christians as "filthy creatures", "disgusting perverts", "damnable sinners" and the like.[79] Rictor Norton puts it even more strongly: "The church's record regarding homosexuals is an atrocity from beginning to end: it is not for us to seek forgiveness, but for the church to make atonement".[80] Peter Tatchell, a well-known British campaigner for gay rights, has said, "The Bible is to gays what *Mein Kampf* is to Jews". It is the theory and practice of "homo holocaust".[81]

Homophobia, the attitude of personal antipathy towards gay people, may be a mixture of irrational fear, hostility and even revulsion.[82] But they deserve our understanding and compassion (though many find this patronising), not our rejection. No wonder Richard Lovelace calls for "a double repentance": not only that sexually active gay Christians

78 Macourt (ed.), *Towards a Theology of Gay Liberation*, p. 63.

79 Pittenger, *Time for Consent*, p. 2.

80 Macourt (ed.), *Towards a Theology of Gay Liberation*, p. 45.

81 See http://www.petertatchell.net/religion/genocide.htm.

82 The word "homophobia" seems to have been used first by George Weinberg in *Society and the Healthy Homosexual* (New York: Doubleday, 1973).

renounce their sexual practice, but also that "straight Christians renounce homophobia."[83] Dr David Atkinson is right to add, "We are not at liberty to urge the Christian homosexual to celibacy and to a spreading of his relationships, unless support for the former and opportunities for the latter are available in genuine love".[84] I rather think that the very existence of groups such as the Lesbian and Gay Christian Movement is a vote of censure on the church.

At the heart of the human condition is a deep and natural hunger for mutual love, a search for identity and a longing for completeness. If gay people cannot find these things in the local "church family", we have no business to go on using that expression. The alternatives are not between the warm, intimate relationship which includes sexual intercourse and the pain of isolation in the cold. There is a third option: namely a Christian environment of love, understanding, acceptance and support. Not all gay people will choose to disclose their sexual inclinations to everybody. But we all need at least one confidant(e) to whom we can unburden ourselves, who will not despise or reject us but will support us with friendship and prayer, and probably offer some private and confidential pastoral counsel. And, like all single people, they will flourish in an environment where they can find many warm and affectionate friendships with people of both sexes.

---

83 Richard R. Lovelace, *Homosexuality and the Church* (Grand Rapids: Revell, 1978), p. 129; cf. p. 125.

84 David J. Atkinson, *Homosexuals in the Christian Fellowship* (Oxford: Latimer House, 1979), p. 118. See also Dr Atkinson's more extensive treatment in his *Pastoral Ethics in Practice* (London: Monarch, 1989). Dr Roger Moss concentrates on pastoral questions in his *Christians and Homosexuality* (Carlisle, Penn.: Paternoster, 1977).

Same-sex friendships, like those in the Bible between Ruth and Naomi, David and Jonathan, and Paul and Timothy, are to be encouraged. There is no hint that any of these was sexual, yet they were evidently affectionate and (at least in the case of David and Jonathan) even demonstrative (for example, 1 Samuel 18:1-4; 20:41; 2 Samuel 1:26). Of course, sensible safeguards will be important. But in some cultures it is common to see two men walking down the street hand in hand, without embarrassment. It is sad that our Western culture inhibits the development of rich same-sex friendships by engendering the fear of being ridiculed or rejected for being gay on the one hand, or by assuming that same-sex intimacy is necessarily sexual on the other.

The best contribution of Michael Vasey's book *Strangers and Friends*, in my view, is his emphasis on friendship. "Friendship is not a minor theme of the Christian faith," he writes, "but is integral to its vision of life".[85] He sees society as "a network of friendships held together by bonds of affection". He also points out that Scripture does "not limit the notion of covenant to the institution of marriage".[86] As David and Jonathan made a covenant with each other (1 Samuel 18:3), we too may have special covenanted friendships.

These and other relationships, both same-sex and opposite-sex, need to be developed within the family of God which, though universal, has its local manifestations. God intends each local church to be a warm, accepting and supportive community. By "accepting" I do not mean accepting of sexual

---

85 Vasey, *Strangers and Friends*, p. 122.
86 *Ibid.*, p. 233.

relationships outside marriage between a man and a woman. No, true love is not incompatible with the maintenance of moral standards. On the contrary, it insists on them, for the good of everybody. There is, therefore, a place for church discipline in the case of members who refuse to repent and wilfully persist in same-sex sexual relationships. But it must be exercised in a spirit of humility and gentleness (Galatians 6:1ff.); we must be careful not to discriminate between men and women or between homosexual and heterosexual offences; and necessary discipline in the case of a public scandal is not to be confused with a witch-hunt.

Perplexing and painful as the homosexual Christian's dilemma is, Jesus Christ offers him or her—indeed, all of us— faith, hope and love: the faith to accept both his standards and his grace to maintain them, the hope to look beyond present suffering to future glory, and the love to care for and support one another. "But the greatest of these is love" (1 Corinthians 13:13).

Ed's Story

Back in the mid-1990s I was an undergraduate at a university college with an evangelical heritage. An ordained staff member had just published a book suggesting that sexually active same-sex relationships were not wrong for Christians. A huge amount of controversy followed.

I sat down and read this revisionist book over the next university vacation; I didn't want to criticise something I hadn't explored for myself with an open mind. I read it as a young Christian not yet open about my own developing same-sex attractions. I had never come across such new ideas before, but both the pain of the author's experience and his odd methods in questioning Scripture and doctrine deeply troubled me. Afterwards, I needed someone who could help me respond with both pastoral compassion and biblical clarity to this book—and to my own personal experience.

I suspect it would have been my dad who would have pointed me in the direction of the latest edition of John Stott's Issues Facing Christians Today and his chapter on homosexuality. There I found someone who clearly loved both the people he was writing about and God's Word. I also benefitted from the insights of an evangelical leader who was not afraid to interact with the ever-developing scientific research in this whole area and those who interpreted the Bible very differently to him.

Looking back, I have John Stott to thank for encouraging me not to seek a same-sex sexual relationship for myself. The characteristically careful distinctions he opens with helped me process my sexual feelings in a liveable way. His exposition of the biblical passages that speak about homosexual practice built my confidence in God's word. His big-picture portrait of the place of marriage in the Bible and Christian doctrine enabled me to make sense of these biblical prohibitions in their wider context. His careful refutations of new interpretations and cultural attitudes exposed the flimsy premises on which they were built. But his clear, pastoral love and concern for people like me also stopped me from feeling steamrollered by the intellectual weight of what he was arguing.

In particular I can remember being moved by how he provocatively challenged his evangelical readers. Towards the end of the chapter Stott makes this incredibly important point:

> At the heart of the human condition is a deep and natural hunger for mutual love, a search for identity and a longing for completeness. If gay people cannot find these things in the local "church family", we have no business to go on using that expression.

This was written by a man who got what it was I was looking for. But it was also written by a man who saw the need to challenge evangelical churches to enable people like me to find these life-giving things in their midst. He rightly saw that repeated talk of "church family" was not enough—it needed to become a lived reality for people like me.

A couple of decades later the ministry of www.livingout.org continues to pose a similar challenge to evangelical churches—

often using Stott's words here. We continue to need to take them seriously, and to use them to help break the all-pervasive idolatry of the nuclear family in society today. Wonderfully they are words that have been taken seriously by many, and I keep hearing of evangelical churches in which gay people are experiencing a genuine family life, warmly welcomed and supported by their sisters and brothers in Christ.

But if that is to become a universal experience, this challenge from Stott needs to be heard again. And its wider context needs to be read too. Interestingly, no significant new territory has been opened up in the Church's protracted discussions on human sexuality since he wrote these words: they continue to speak with relevance into our contemporary debates.

I am so grateful to John Stott for the guidance he gave me as a young same-sex attracted Christian over twenty years ago. He helped keep me on a course that has enabled me to grow in Christ and flourish as a human being. I am delighted that this new edition will give others the chance to benefit from his wisdom and insight—and it's my hope and prayer that many will be encouraged to further embrace the life-giving teaching of God in Jesus Christ.

Ed Shaw is the pastor of Emmanuel City Centre in Bristol and a trustee of www.livingout.org.

Questions for Reflection and Discussion

1. Has your church taken steps to communicate to gay people that they are welcome, and to ensure that the members who are gay or experience same-sex attraction feel safe and comfortable enough to be open about their sexuality?

2. How do you think the church can best welcome and support gay people and other sexual minorities?

3. Read/watch some of the testimonies and stories on the True Freedom Trust (https://truefreedomtrust.co.uk/stories) and Living Out (http://www.livingout.org/stories) websites. Are there particular lessons about friendship and pastoral care which can be learned from them?

4. Regardless of your own sexual orientation, how would you respond if someone came out to you?

5. What does Genesis 2:4-25 teach us about heterosexual marriage and how is this reinforced by Jesus in Matthew 19:4-7? Is there any room within this framework for a

biblical endorsement of a lifelong same-sex partnership?

6. What do you think is the purpose of sex within God's creation?

7. To what extent do you think this is an issue about which Christians can agree to disagree?

8. Read over the "real lives" sections again. What insight do these stories give you into the lives of believers who are living with same-sex attraction? How might you have supported them, or someone like them, when they were at the point of wrestling with their questions about sexuality and Christian commitment? How could you be supporting someone now?

9. In the time between 1984, when John Stott originally wrote this chapter, and now, what do you think has changed? And what do you think has stayed the same?

thegoodbook
COMPANY

BIBLICAL | RELEVANT | ACCESSIBLE

At The Good Book Company, we are dedicated to helping Christians and local churches grow. We believe that God's growth process always starts with hearing clearly what he has said to us through his timeless word—the Bible.

Ever since we opened our doors in 1991, we have been striving to produce resources that honour God in the way the Bible is used. We have grown to become an international provider of user-friendly resources to the Christian community, with believers of all backgrounds and denominations using our Bible studies, books, evangelistic resources, DVD-based courses and training events.

We want to equip ordinary Christians to live for Christ day by day, and churches to grow in their knowledge of God, their love for one another, and the effectiveness of their outreach.

Call us for a discussion of your needs or visit one of our local websites for more information on the resources and services we provide.

Your friends at The Good Book Company

UK & EUROPE   thegoodbook.co.uk   0333 123 0880
NORTH AMERICA thegoodbook.com 866 244 2165
AUSTRALIA thegoodbook.com.au (02) 9564 3555
NEW ZEALAND thegoodbook.co.nz (+64) 3 343 2463

WWW.CHRISTIANITYEXPLORED.ORG
Our partner site is a great place for those exploring the Christian faith, with a clear explanation of the good news, powerful testimonies and answers to difficult questions.